The Magic of Attitude

Success Strategies for Finding Magic in the Cards you are Dealt

ERIC ANDERSON

Copyright © 2023 The Magic of Attitude Publishing

All rights reserved.

No part of this publication may be reproduced or transmitted in any form or by any means, mechanical or electronic, including photocopying and recording, or by any information storage and retrieval system, without permission in writing from the author or publisher (except by reviewer, who may quote brief passages and/or show brief video clips in a review).

Disclaimer: The Publisher and the Author make no representations or warranties with respect to the accuracy or completeness or the contents of this work and specifically disclaim all warranties, including without limitation warranties of fitness for a particular purpose. No warranty may be created or extended by sales or promotional materials. The advice and strategies contained herein may not be suitable for every situation. This work is sold with the understanding that the Publisher is not engaged in rendering legal, accounting, or other professional services. If professional assistance is required, the services of the competent professional person should be sought. The fact that an organization or website is referred to in this work as a citation and/or a potential source of further information does not mean that the Author or the Publisher endorses the information the organization or website may provide or recommendations it may make. Further, readers should be aware that internet websites listed in this work may have changed or disappeared between when this work was written and when it is read.

Published by:

Magic of Attitude Publishing

To inquire about Eric Anderson's *LIVE EVENTS* please use the information below.

Magic of Attitude
2260 Fairburn Rd #311547
Atlanta, Georgia 31131
Office (404) 286-2973
Eric@EricTylerAnderson.com

Eric's Acknowledgments

I'd like to thank my children Samantha and Sebastian, who are my biggest fans. Being their father has allowed me to reach new levels in my life while opening me up to the importance of having a family that truly loves you.

Thanks to everyone that has impacted my life for the better; without you crossing my path at some point I would not be the person I am today.

To all of the youth that have experienced life in the foster care system, you are my heroes.

Eric Anderson
The Magician with a Message

Other Acknowledgements

"All our dreams can come true...if we have the courage to pursue them."
                              Walt Disney

Contents

Introduction	6
The Magic of Attitude Success Strategy #1	10
The Magic of Goal Setting Success Strategy #2	20
The Magic of Time Management Success Strategy #3	34
The Magic of Perception Success Strategy #4	43
Summary of Success Strategies	52
Good Reads	56
Words of Wisdom from Eric Anderson	57
About Eric Anderson	60
Getting Unstuck	65
Magical Resources	72

Introduction

We cannot change the cards we are dealt, just how we play the hand. - Randy Paush

I am a former foster youth. I've been in the trenches and have survived.

- I entered foster care at 9 years old
- I aged out of foster care at 18 years old
- I lived in 6 foster homes
- I attended 4 high schools
- I lived through different types of abuse, even homelessness

And yet my life has been "Magical." Every day I have the opportunity to travel the world doing something I love. And now as a husband and father, I teach my children every lesson I wish I would have been taught growing up. I wrote this book to provide key information that will help foster youth to succeed.

My personal definition of success is:

"Live your life by design and not by default"

The pages that follow will provide success strategies to help you achieve your goals.

Let's get started.

THE MAGIC IN THE CARDS YOU ARE DEALT

The Magic of Attitude
Success Strategy # 1

The moment you accept responsibility for everything in your life, is the moment you can change anything in your life. -
Yo Pal" Hal Elrod

The Blame Game

For a number of years I was a chronic blamer. I could play the blame game better then Michael Jordan played basketball.

- I blamed my adoptive father for abusing me.

- I blamed him again for putting me in foster care.

- I blamed the foster families I lived with for not treating me well.

THE MAGIC IN THE CARDS YOU ARE DEALT

- I blamed the Child Welfare System for not teaching me to succeed.

- I blamed everyone for everything.

- I blamed everybody but the person who deserved the bland--- and that was me.

Oh yeah, I could go on and on about my situation--- how I was abused and how that gave me a reason to act out--- but the truth is, if I knew enough to pass the blame on someone else then that meant I recognized that I had a problem and needed a solution. Knowing that I had a problem put the responsibility on me to change my situation.

Regardless of whether or not I have the correct answers to solve the problem at hand, the simple fact that I know I have a problem puts the responsibility on me to change my situation.

We live in a time where people refuse to take responsibility for their lives and would rather play the blame game. Today I refuse to play that game.

My attitude has changed drastically for the better. Instead of blaming the world for the challenges I have, and will continue to have in my life, I'd rather pick myself up, take a look in the mirror, and say, "It's up to me."

Today I understand that playing the blame game is an excuse for not taking action. Even if I don't know what to do, I still know that I must be doing something. If I can control my attitude, then I can control my life.

Life in Control

I developed and followed a three step process to get my life in control.

1. I Understand that every action I take has a result. Sometimes that

result is good and sometimes it's bad, but there is always a result. **ALWAYS!**

2. I Ask myself this question: "What is the end result of the action I'm about to take?"

3. I Determine whether or not I can live with the result. If my answer is yes, I move forward. If my answer is no, I can make another choice.

> Also, if I choose to take an action and I know the answer is NO (I cannot live with the result) and I take that action anyway, I know I'm acting irresponsibly and I must face the music.

It's important to understand that the end result is not what you think it is. Let me explain with a story.

The Rent is Due

After aging out of foster care I found myself in a situation in which I could not pay my rent. Since I was never schooled in what to do if you do not have your rent, a few thought popped up about how I could get the money. I reasoned that the most practical method to raise the money would be to snatch a few purses until I had the money I needed to pay my rent. I played this scenario in my head a few times until I reasoned that the real result would not be me getting the money to pay my rent, but the real result would be me going to jail for robbery.

Read that last sentence again. The REAL RESULT would be me possibly going to jail for robbery. Since that was not the result I wanted to live with, I made a better choice. Here is what I did.

>I went to the manager of my apartment building and told her I did

The Magic of Attitude

not have the rent and how soon I would have to be out. She asked me when I would have all of the rent. I told her I would have it in about two weeks because that's when I get paid.

She responded with, "Great. When you get paid in two weeks, bring your rent with an additional 10% for a late payment charge." I literally looked at her in disbelief and asked her if that was all I had to do. She said, "That's it."

I was blown away. That was one of the moments that changed my life. I was about to possibly ruin my life over a few hundred dollars and all I had to do was ask a question.

I learned that practically every challenge that I would be faced with in life already has a solution. All I have to do is discover the solution. As simple as that may seem, it's actually profound.

From that day forward, my life changed. My attitude changed when I discovered that even if I did not have the answer I knew someone else had already done the homework for me. All I had to do was find the answer(s).

Anger Management

During a Q & A portion of my presentation for youth living in a group home I was asked how I control my temper when someone makes me **MAD.**

Here's how I responded

First, I acknowledge that I get **"*annoyed*"** at certain things. But I ultimately choose how I'm going to respond. I was in numerous situations in which I really got upset about something and I acted like a fool. After one of my episodes I played the scene over and over and realized how stupid I looked.

At that moment I understood I was raising my voice as a self-defense mechanism. I figured that the louder I was and the more I acted out, the more power I thought I had. The simple truth is that I was out of control and I looked like a coward. In fact, it is rare that the loudest person in the room is the most confident. Often he has the most to hide and that's why he is being so loud.

I changed how I saw myself in these situations. If I wasn't being powerful, I was really showing how weak I was because I was allowing someone or something else to influence my behavior.

The Rules of a Magical Attitude

I live by three simple rules:

Rule 1 – Be Natural

Dai Vernon, the Greatest Sleight of Hand magician of the twentieth century, stated that in performing sleight of hand magic one must Be Natural. He said when you make unnatural movements while performing you expose what you're trying to hide. Of course he is talking about sleight of hand magic, but that same principle applies to succeeding in life.

Rule 2 – Take the Ego Out of the Equation

When I conducted my own self therapy, I found that for every problem in which my ego was involved, I found it more difficult to find workable solutions. When I removed my ego –- problem solved.

Rule 3 – Bullet Proof

As long as I know I'm doing the right thing, I could care less what other people think about me. I am bullet proof to negative thoughts concerning how other people perceive me. My major responsibility in life is not to let my family down.

Remember, when you control your attitude, you control your life and ultimately you make better choices.

NOTES - The Magic of Attitude

If you want your life to be more rewarding, you have to change the way you think
- *Oprah Winfrey*

The Magic of Goal Setting
Success Strategy #2

The moment you begin to think like a winner then you will become one. – Valerie Parker

Imagine you had a magic wand that you could wave and produce anything you want in your life. The difference between succeeding and failure is vision. If you're able to see, feel, and emotionalize what you want, your odds of getting it increase a hundred fold. You experience life based on where you focus your attention. I am referring to goal setting.

This success principle is so simple; I'm shocked more people don't apply it in their lives. I believe the reason more people don't apply the principle of goal setting in their lives is because they don't know how to apply it. Or they have heard the concept but don't understand there is a formal process to turn their goals into real life experiences.

The Car

The very first time I put the Magic of Goal setting into action in my life was after reading *Think and Grow Rich* by Napoleon Hill. He outlines how to get whatever you want.

I was living in San Diego and needed a car. I had very little money - definitely not enough money for down payment on a new car and not enough money to buy a used car. All I knew is I needed a car. I followed the step by step process that was laid out in Hill's book. I wrote down lots of goals but the car was just one of them. As Mr. Hill mentioned in his book, when you become aware of what you want, you start to notice opportunities are all around you just begging you to take advantage of them.

The next day I found myself in a conversation with a complete stranger in a restaurant. During this conversation he mention he had a Toyota that he wasn't sure what he was going to do with it. I asked him if he thought about selling the car. He said no. Out of the blue I said, "If you're willing to accept a few payments over the next few months I will buy the Toyota from you." He asked how much money I could put down on the car and I told him about $75.00 dollars. To my surprise, he agreed to my terms and we set up a time to meet the next day so I could pick up the car and start making payments. What is great about this story is I did not use the other step outlined in *Think & Grow Rich.* All I did was:

- Become aware that I needed a car

- Believe that I was going to get a car

- Noticed an opportunity

Since then I have used a more refined process to make life happen by writing books, starting business, paying off debt, traveling the world, and living life on my own terms. If you did nothing else and simply wrote down a list of what you wanted, you would achieve most of the stuff on that list by simply making yourself aware.

Let me explain the step-by-step process I use today to put things in motion to achieve some of my life's dreams. My system is a hybrid of what I have read and applied over the years.

Goal Setting Steps

Review the steps outlined below and then begin using the worksheet I have included on pages 31 – 32

Step 1 – Dream about everything you want to do, be, and achieve while you are on this planet and write these dreams down on a piece of paper. It's important that you do not edit your thinking. By that I mean don't write something and then erase it and say I can't do that. I'm giving you the license to dream big.

Write down everything and write really fast. As you are writing it's important to think about these four categories.

1. **Career (C)**
2. **Giving Back (G)**
3. **Toys (T)**
4. **Personal (P)**

That's the first step. Write until you can't write anymore.

Step 2 - Once you have your master list you want to go through each goal and put a C, G, T, or P next to each one of your written goals. These letters stand for Career, Giving Back, Toys, and Personal.

The Magic of Attitude

THE MAGIC IN THE CARDS YOU ARE DEALT

Now go through your master list and choose one goal for each category. You will have four goals.

Step 3 – Take these four goals and for each one write down the exact goal you are going to achieve. For example, if your goal is to make more money, instead of just writing *"more money,"* you must come up with an exact amount of money you are going to make. If your goal is to give back to your community, you must come up with an organization and exactly what you are going to do for them.

Step 4 - Write down how you are going to reward yourself for achieving this goal. Make sure it's something fun and exciting. Now for something radically different from the majority of goal achieving systems, you must write down the consequence for not achieving your attended goal. The *Reward and Consequence Factor* will help keep you on track and moving forward.

Step 5 - Write down today's date or the exact date you will start the process of achieving this goal. Now you must also write down your deadline date. This is the timeframe in which you will achieve your goal. It's important to recognize that even though you might have a timeframe of 6 months to accomplish your goal it might only take you one month. Remember this - you will accomplish your goals at the exact timeframe that you set for yourself.

Step 6 - Write a paragraph about why you must achieve the goal at hand. You **MUST** have a compelling reason why you are going to achieve your goal. Without enough positive reasons **WHY**, you will never put the energy into moving towards your dreams. If the **WHY** is strong enough, you will do what it takes to accomplish your goal.

Step 7 - Write down each and every step you must take to make your goal a reality.

There are only so many steps to reach any given goal on your master list. This last step is important because you are about to map out your path to success. Here is exactly what you must do:

> Do not try to write down the steps in order. You can put them in order later; for now just write down what steps you think you might take towards accomplishing this goal. For example, if your goal is to purchase a new car, one of your steps would be to decide exactly what type of car you want. Another step would be taking the care for a test drive. Another step might be finding out how much you need for a down payment. Think of these steps as minor actions that lead to major results. Once you have all of your steps written down on paper you want to put them into a logical order. Don't worry about missing a step because that missed step will

make itself apparent when you reach that point on your list.

You now have an exact road map for achieving your goals.

You will want to follow Steps 1 - 7 for each one of your goals out of the four you chose from your master list. As you achieve each goal, you must replace it with another goal from that category to keep your progress moving forward.

You will want to always make sure you are achieving goals in each of the four categories I mentioned. This way you will always be moving toward balance in your life. Often times your life will get out of balance and that's OK. At least this way you are aware when you are out of sync and you can start putting yourself back in balance.

Your Purpose in Life Statement

THE MAGIC IN THE CARDS YOU ARE DEALT

You must create your purpose in life statement. On a small laminated card that I keep in my wallet is my purpose in life statement. The front side has the following paragraph printed on it.

***My purpose in life** - I was put on this planet to improve every area of my life. Each and every day I'm on this planet I will live my life with love, energy, and fun. I will share the knowledge I have learned about succeeding against the odds. I will do everything in my power to be a living role model for my family and for those who choose to follow my path. The day that I leave this planet I hope to receive a standing ovation because I lived with passion, I loved people, and most importantly I gave back! That's the purpose of my life!*

The other side has the four goals I'm moving towards on a small post-it note attached to the card. My job is to keep this card with me and read the statement followed by reading my goals at least once a day.

This will have a powerful impact on how you feel and, equally important, it will keep your goals on the forefront of your mind. With your goals always on your mind you will start to notice opportunity all around you.

I don't believe in complicating the process. I use a simple notebook for my goals because I prefer to physically write out my goals and I suggest you do the same.

There you have it, a simple yet **POWERFUL** system for accomplishing anything you can dream for yourself.

The next success strategy will show you how to incorporate The Magic of Time Management into your daily life.

Worksheet - The Magic of Goal Setting

1. List your goals (dreams)

2. Assign a category to each goal: Career (C), Giving Back (G), Toys (T), Personal (P)

3. Identify the exact goal you are going to achieve

Worksheet
The Magic of Goal Setting (continued)

4. Write how you will reward yourself for achieving the goal and the consequence for not achieving your goal

5. List start and stop dates for the goal

6. Write a paragraph about why you must achieve the goal

7. Write the steps needed to reach the goal

NOTES - The Magic of Goal Setting

You have the power to be, do, or create anything you choose. You are an infinite being with unlimited potential - Gail Lynne Goodwin

The Magic of Time Management
Success Strategy # 3

"If you are killing time, it's not murder. It's suicide." -**Lou Holtz**

Life is not fair and I doubt that will ever change. Blaming the world for the disadvantage I was born with is a waste of time. The one advantage we all are given is the amount of time we have on this planet. Of course the amount changes from person to person, but what you do with the time you are given will ultimately determine your success or failure.

I'm amazed at what people can accomplish even though they are born with disadvantages. On the other side of that coin, I'm always surprised when I experience someone who was born with major advantages and choose to slowly let their life pass them by.

If someone gives me a rundown of what they do in any given week, I bet I could predict the outcome of their life and I bet I would get fairly close.

Moments of Time

There were two moments in my life in which I began to respect my time.

The First Moment - I was seventeen years old and a friend of mine was going to come pick me up so we could hang out that night. He wanted me to wait outside so I could wave at him when he approached since it was really dark in the area and he was not familiar with that part of town. We talked on the phone and he mentioned he was leaving and he would be there in about 30 - 45 minutes. I waited for about twenty minutes and then went outside to continue waiting. This was well before cell phones became popular so I just had to wait and wait and wait. He drove up ninety minutes late from his estimated time of arrival. Naturally I figured something had happened.

When he arrived I asked what happened and he said nothing; he just left a little later than expected. He acted like it was not a problem. I was livid and told myself in that moment I would never waste my time or disrespect the time of other people.

This person was and still is habitually late. The sad thing is he blames the world for his personal challenges, when the simple truth is he just doesn't show up.

The Second Moment - My former Social Worker, Charles Russell, who is the brother of basketball legend Bill Russell, sat me down and did something that impacted my life in a major way. He scheduled my entire day from beginning to end. My entire schedule was mapped out for me. It's kind of hard to get in trouble when you are supposed to be doing something productive.

I have taken this same principle of scheduling everything and applied it to my life and it's a wickedly powerful success strategy.

Some people choose to be late rather than be early. The motivation usually stems from not wanting to be perceived as corny for being on time. My rule is if you're not early you are late. Period!

Also, I know some really successful people who will not even consider you as an option for anything if you're late. They will judge everything about who you are as a person because you are late. The other way of looking at it is, if someone doesn't respect their own time why would they respect yours?

Let's take it one step further; your time is your life and do you really want to be around someone who doesn't respect your life. ? It's a little harsh, but think about it for a second.

11 Successful Time Management Secrets

- Schedule everything; get in the habit of putting everything on your calendar.

- Plan your entire day from beginning to end. Move to planning your week, then your month, then your entire year.

- Spend less time with people who waste time.

- Create a **Things to Do** list. Write down a daily list of everything you must accomplish that day.

- Create a **Things Not To Do** list. When I first thought of the concept of taking an honest look at everything I was doing to waste my own time and actively took steps to not do these things, I create more time for myself.

- Focus on making the process fun, but remember the results are what truly matter.

- Arrive at least 30 minutes early to everything.

- Write one of your action steps from your magic of goal setting system onto the things to do list.

- Just get started. Never worry about having everything perfect.

- Learn how to focus. If I could get more people into the habit of working uninterrupted for 2-3 hours,

I could show anyone how to succeed.

- Be flexible. Stuff will come up that is not on your schedule and that's OK as long as you complete the task at hand.

"When I was really young, I did not complete a chore given to me. I was told to write one thousand times."

WHEN I START SOMETHING I WILL FINISH IT

Trust me when I say that the idea of completing something after starting it is hard wired into my system.

THE MAGIC IN THE CARDS YOU ARE DEALT

NOTES - The Magic of Time Management

Be not afraid of going slowly; be only afraid of standing still - Chinese Proverb

Notes

The Magic of Perception

The Magic of Attitude

Success Strategy # 4

Positive action cures everything, it always does, and it always will - Bradley Quick

I was speaking with a group of foster youth who were about to age out of the system and start living on their own. One of the young ladies in the group had a question. She asked how do I get people to stop passing judgment on me and at least give me a chance. That was a great question and I have the perfect answer that has been tested over and over again.

The one thing that I learned from the art of magic is how to change people's perceptions. If you change how people perceive you, then your odds of success increase. People are going to judge you regardless so you might as well give them something to judge.

Before I reveal what I believe to be one of the most powerful success strategies you can employ when dealing with other people, let me share 4 stories about perception.

4 Stories on Perception

Story 1 -- I was living in San Diego when this happened to me. There was a big group of people who - including myself - jaywalked across the street. Please keep in mind I was not with any of the others in this group. A police officer yelled to me, "Hey, stop and come here." I did. He told me I crossed the street illegally and he was going to give me a ticket. I said, "The entire group jaywalked. Why did you single me out?" Without skipping a beat he said, "Those people have some place to be."

Story 2 -- I had just finished working out at the gym. I decided to go to the store before I headed back to my office. Since I did not have any cash on me I decided to use a check to pay for the items I was taking back to the office. I handed the cashier the check. She looked me up and down and said she would not be able to process the check. I asked why and she called for the manager. He said it was a business check. I said, "I know. I'm the owner of the business." He looked me up and down with a look of disgust on his face and said, "You own a business? Yeah right!" He refused to accept my check even though I gave him everything he asked for.

Story 3 -- My wife and I were headed to California for a vacation. We arrived to the airport to long lines and delays. After standing in one of these lines, an airport employee picks me out of the group of at least 100 people standing in this line. She starts a new line with me being the head of this line. As a matter of fact, she walked past a lot of people to choose me.
Story 4 -- At a conference, the CEO of a huge insurance company offered me a

job with a guaranteed salary of $250,000 per year.

So what's going on? I'm sure there are a number of reasons why you think these situations happened to me. I know exactly why they happened.

I made a simple change that created the change in how people perceived me. In stories 3 and 4, I put on a suit. That's right - I simply changed my clothing and I looked like someone who had a place to go and things to do.

We always tell people not to judge a book by its cover. On the surface it sounds like great advice but the problem is that is not how the world works. People judge books by the cover all the time. If that's true −and it is − you want to be in control of what they judge.
The fastest and simplest way that I know how to change someone's perception of you is to put on your good clothes.

THE MAGIC IN THE CARDS YOU ARE DEALT

My strategy is simple – always dress like I've come from some place nicer and I'm going somewhere better. When people start to ask you where you just came from or where you are going, you will know you are on the right track

When you put your good clothes on:

- You feel better about yourself

- You walk with a little more pep in your step.

- You tend to hold your head higher.

- Your attitude changes for the better.

Most people only dress up for special occasions. As far as I'm concerned, every day above the ground is a Special Occasion.

Let's take one final look at perception.

The Story of Juan

The first time I recognized this principle at work was in high school. A friend of mine named Juan always came to school in suits every day. I mean every single day. The teachers treated him with more respect than the rest of us. All the other students thought he was the go-to guy when they need help. If there was a situation at school, he was automatically excluded from the group because the teachers knew he had nothing to do with it because he was dressed up.

One day I asked Juan why he dressed in suits every day. He told me his father told him it would make his life easier.

I'm not sure what Juan is doing today but I would guess he is successful.

10 Day Challenge

Put on your best clothes for 10 days straight. Take notice how people treat you during those 10 days. Jot down responses to the following questions:

- What did you notice?

- How did it make you feel?

- What did you learn?

In life you get ahead by standing out. This is the easiest way to stand out in the world because nobody is doing it.

Those that do will reap the rewards.

NOTES - The Magic of Perception

Never allow others to define your potential

- *Marjorie Brody*

Notes

THE MAGIC IN THE CARDS YOU ARE DEALT

Summary of Success Strategies

The Magic of Attitude

- ❏ Be Natural
- ❏ Take the Ego Out of the Equation
- ❏ Bullet Proof

The Magic of Goal Setting

- ❏ List your goals (dreams)
- ❏ Assign a category to each goal: Career, Giving Back, Toys, Personal
- ❏ Identify the exact goal you are going to achieve
- ❏ Determine how you will reward yourself for achieving the goal and the consequence for not achieving your goal
- ❏ List start and stop dates for the goal

❑ Write a paragraph about why you must achieve the goal

❑ Write steps needed to reach the goal

The Magic of Time Management

11 Successful Time Management Secrets

1. Schedule everything; get in the habit of putting everything on your calendar.

2. Plan your entire day from beginning to end. Move to planning your week, then your month, then your entire year.

3. Spend less time with people who waste time.

4. Create a **Things to Do** list. Write down a daily list of everything you must accomplish that day.

5. Create a **Things Not To Do** list. Write down those things that may waste time.

6. Focus on making the process fun, but remember the results are what truly matter.

7. Arrive at least 30 minutes early to everything.

8. Write one of your action steps from your magic of goal setting system onto the things to do list.

9. Just get started. Never worry about having everything perfect.

10. Learn how to focus uninterrupted for 2-3 hours.

11. Be flexible.

The Magic of Perception

❏ 10 Day Challenge

THE MAGIC IN THE CARDS YOU ARE DEALT

Good Reads

How to Get Out of Your Own Way

by Tyrese Gibson

Think and Grow Rich by Napoleon Hill

Don't Sweat the Small Stuff for Teens; Simple Ways to Keep Your Cool in Stressful Times by Richard Carlson

Words of Wisdom from Eric Anderson

The Magic of Attitude

THE MAGIC IN THE CARDS YOU ARE DEALT

1. Sometimes you have to do something you don't want to do in order to do what you want to do.

2. Here is what I know about failure. You have just learned one more thing that doesn't work, which means you're one step closer to success.

3. If I know enough not to pass the blame to someone else then that means I recognize I have problem that needs to be addressed. It's my responsibility to change my situation.

4. Practically every challenge you will be faced with in life already has a practical solution that has been worked out for you. It's just a matter of asking for the answer.

5. As long as I know I'm doing the right thing I could care less what

other people think about me. I am bullet proof to negative thoughts concerning how other people perceive me.

6. There are opportunities all around you just begging you to take advantage of them.

7. Without enough positive reasons WHY you need to achieve your goal, you will never put the energy into moving towards your dreams.

8. The advantage we all are given is the amount of time we have on this planet. What you do with the time will ultimately determine your success or failure.

9. The fastest and simplest way that I know to change someone's perception of you is to put on your good clothes.

THE MAGIC IN THE CARDS YOU ARE DEALT

10. You experience life based on where you focus your attention.

About Eric Anderson

Eric Anderson was put up for adoption when he was born. He was adopted at the age of two, but because he was being abused, he was removed from his adoptive home and put into the Child Welfare System.

He lived in foster homes and group homes until he was eighteen years old.

Eric firmly believes there is always something positive you can take from every negative situation. One of the fires his adoptive father lit in him was his love for the art of magic. After receiving a magic set one year for Christmas, Eric became fascinated with this art form. Even though he lived in a variety of foster homes, he was able to take this special gift with him to help keep him focused. With hard work and a determination to succeed, Eric has become one of the best magicians in the world.
When he turned eighteen he realized he was going to start living on his own and

he remembered something his Social Worker told him.

He said— *"Eric do you realize if you put the same effort and energy into your school work like you do with your magic, school would be a breeze?"*

He didn't listen to his Social Worker, but years later Eric took that same idea and applied it to his life.

After aging out of foster care he served a brief stint in the United States Air Force. Moving back to San Diego, he did everything from drive a cab to entertain people on the streets to make extra money.

Realizing he needed to change his environment and start from scratch, Eric put everything he owned in one bag and bought a one way ticket on a Grey Hound bus from San Diego to Atlanta. After arriving in Atlanta he went to work changing his life for the better.

There were a couple of setbacks, like HOMELESSNESS, but he was able to pick up the pieces of his life and he kept moving towards his goals.

Eric realized he already had the skills to succeed, all he had to do was apply those skills to other areas of his life. That's exactly what he did.

Eric started a business that designed and produced magically themed events for corporations worldwide. In addition to producing events for two Super Bowls and the Olympics, he has shared the platform with Talk Show Host Sean Hannity, First Lady Laura Bush, Home Run King Hank Aaron, and Nobel Peace Prize recipient and former President of the United States Jimmy Carter. He was selected to perform at the "Salute to Heroes Inaugural Ball" during President

THE MAGIC IN THE CARDS YOU ARE DEALT

Barack Obama's Inauguration in Washington D.C.

A number of years ago a friend suggested Eric share his story with social workers, foster parents, and youth in foster care.

He made the decision to help youth in foster care by appearing at select events around the nation to talk about what it really takes to succeed after living in foster care.

Even though magicians are known for keeping secrets, Eric is willing to share one of life's greatest secrets How to Live a Magical Life. Eric is internationally recognized as *"The Magician with a Message"* and his list of clients reads like a who's who. He has been in the trenches and survived. Eric Anderson is a perfect example of Art Imitating Life.

Today Eric is married to his wife Monique and still lives in Atlanta, Georgia.

Notes

Getting Unstuck

Basic effect: Audience puts their hands together in the prayer position and they are unable to separate their third fingers.

THE MAGIC IN THE CARDS YOU ARE DEALT

The effect is extremely simple: Put your hands together in the prayer position. (See figure 1.) When you turn your middle fingers in on themselves all of a sudden it becomes almost impossible to separate your third fingers.

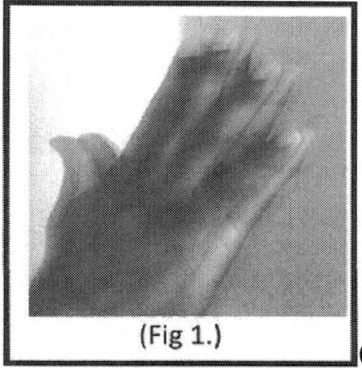

(Fig 1.)

Couple this basic effect with a presentation- now you have something you can use to communicate a message to foster youth.

Most people who have learned this childhood stunt know the version in which you put your band on the table and turn the middle finger down on the table. This version allows you to perform this for an entire audience and the demonstration plays huge.

What you're about to learn is one of the simplest yet most powerful pieces I use in my professional repertoire. It is strictly a presentation piece. This is my presentation for a very old effect that I read in Martin Gardner's Impromptu Magic. I sure most have tried this at some point and ignored it. I have used this routine close-up, on stage, and on television. The effect will work for ANY type of performance venue and allows you to communicate a message in the process.

And you don't need anything with you. This particular presentation is the one I use for my Magic with a Message programs.

THE MAGIC IN THE CARDS YOU ARE DEALT

What I'm sharing with you now is the presentation I use most often.

"Everybody hold your hands out like so: palms out, palms in palm. Great, now put your hands together and hold your hands in front of you like so. Before we start, there are only three rules to remember. First rule: you can only move one set of fingers at a time. The second rule is you must keep your other finger tips together as you move that set of .fingers. And the third rule is remembering the first two rules, OK? Before we start, let's make sure everything is working OK. Hold your hands in, front of you."

> 1. *Separate your thumbs; now put your thumbs back.*
> 2. *Separate your pinkies; now put your pinkies back.*
> 3. *Separate your first fingers; now put your fingers back.*
> 4. *Separate your middle fingers; now put your middle fingers back.*

5. Separate your third, fingers; now put your third fingers back.

Is everything working OK? Great! We are going to talk about four important life concepts. And since we are only talking about four concepts, I want you to turn your middle fingers down like this. Those are negative fingers and today we are not going to deal with anything negative. Let's continue- I want you to imagine for a moment you have the world's best attitude. Nothing can bother you and you keep this incredible attitude between your thumbs. Fantastic! Next I want you to think about all of your dreams and goals; everything you want to do, be, and achieve, and imagine you keep these dreams between your first fingers. Great!

Next I want you to think about your ego and your insecurities; everything you're afraid for other people to find out about you. Imagine you keep these thoughts between your third fingers. Next, I want you think about your motivation. These

THE MAGIC IN THE CARDS YOU ARE DEALT

are the things or thoughts that keep you inspired and moving in the right direction. Is everyone with me? Say, "yes."

OK, let's role play for a moment. Life is going great! You're living your dream life, you're inspired, you're at a perfect place mentally, and then something happens. It's going to change from person to person, but whatever this something is, it bothers you; it eats at your core and all of a sudden you lose this fantastic attitude. To represent that idea, everyone separate your thumbs; now put your thumbs back. That represents you losing your great attitude.

As soon as you lose your great attitude your motivation starts to slip. To represent that idea, separate your pinkies and put your pinkies back. You just lost your motivation; when you lose your motivation, your dreams and goals are not going to happen.

To represent that idea, *separate your first fingers put your first fingers back. You just threw away your dreams and goals. The only thing you're holding onto now is your ego and insecurities. On three, everyone separate your third fingers. See how challenging that is? All of a sudden, we, find ourselves stuck. You see how easy it is to let go of things that help us and hold onto things that hurt us.*

Here is the first step I take when I need to get unstuck. I put my ego in check; I take my ego out of the equation. As soon as I do that I'm already closer to a solution. When I'm close to the answer, my attitude goes from good to great. When my attitude is in the right place, I take massive action on my dreams. When I take action on my dreams, I'm inspired. Separate your hands and relax your fingers."

It's important to remember that this is not a Magic effect; this is simply a method to deliver a message, but it presents that message in an entertaining and memorable manner.

Notes

Magical Resources

- www.celebrationofexcellence.org

- www.georgiailp.org

- www.giftforachild.org

- www.thenf.org

- www.reallifeprep.org

- www.highereducationinstitute.org

- www.interfaithchildrensmovement.org

- ww.maac4kids.org/empowerment

- www.gabar.org

- www.erictyleranderson.com

$997.00 Presentation Voucher

With this form, you are entitled to a $997.00 credit when you book one of Eric Anderson's presentations. Because each organizations exact needs are always different when you contact our office for more information

THE MAGIC IN THE CARDS YOU ARE DEALT

we will ask you a few questions concerning your event. From there we will send you a Success Blueprint outlining your options. After you review your options if Eric is a good fit for what you have planned mentioned promo code
pres-997 so we can apply this credit to the overall investment.

Contact our office at
Office (404) 286-2973
eric@erictyleranderson.com

www.EricTylerAnderson.com

Tell us about your life and the magic in the cards you were dealt.

Email us at
office@erictyleranderson.com

Contact Eric Anderson and

share your Magical Life!

Magic of Attitude
2260 Fairburn Rd #311547
Atlanta, GA 30331

Office (404) 286-2973

eric@erictyleranderson.com
Visit us online at
www.EricTylerAnderson.com